BIG · WORK MACHINES

BY PATRICIA RELF
ILLUSTRATED BY TOM LAPADULA

A GOLDEN BOOK · NEW YORK
Western Publishing Company, Inc.
Racine, Wisconsin 53404

Big work machines help people do big jobs. Hundreds of workers digging with handshovels could not dig a big hole as fast as an excavator can. A bulldozer pushes the loose rock and dirt into mounds. Then a front loader carries the mounds of dirt and rock to a dump truck to be hauled away. This enormous hole will hold the foundation of a tall office building.

dump truck

front loader

excavator

bulldozer

sonic hammer

To keep the walls of the hole from caving in, the builders drive in steel beams called piles. A sonic hammer vibrates each pile as it drives the pile deep into the earth. In just a few minutes, a beam as tall as a three-story house has been pushed into the ground.

trencher

Pipes for water and gas, and big electrical cables, will lead into the new building's basement. A trencher cuts right through streets and sidewalks to dig ditches for the pipes and cables. A special pipe-laying crane gently lowers pipes into the ground.

pipe-laying crane

truck crane

    Steel beams have to be hoisted to build the skyscraper's frame. A truck crane can lift heavy loads more than 300 feet in the air. A worker called a rigger hooks up the load, then points two fingers upward to tell the operator to start hoisting.

As the skyscraper gets taller, a taller crane is needed to reach the top floors. A tower crane grows with the building. Workers add new sections near the top of the crane to make it taller. The giant crane hoists steel beams, wooden planks, loads of concrete, and anything else the construction workers need at the top of the new building. The operator uses a radio to talk with workers on the ground and in the building.

tower crane

The skyscraper is nearly finished. Workers begin to take down the enormous crane, one section at a time. Small cranes on the roof help to lower the pieces.

Soon subway trains will run here, right under busy city streets. Workers dig the new tunnel without disturbing the traffic above, using a tunnel-boring machine, or mole.

The mole inches forward, cutting through the rock with dozens of small, sharp, spinning disks. A little train carries the rock and dirt back to the mouth of the tunnel. A beam of light called a laser shows the operator how to steer so that the tunnel will be absolutely straight.

mole

gantry crane

At the harbor, a ship brings in its cargo. A tall gantry crane unloads the big crates. Sitting in the cab high above the ship's deck, the operator can look down at the cargo he is lifting. Trucks—and even a bus full of visitors—can drive between the crane's long legs.

After the cargo is unloaded, it is stored in harbor warehouses. Forklift trucks carry crates to the warehouses and stack them up on shelves. Some forklifts can reach shelves 40 feet high, with the operator sitting in a cab on the ground. Other forklifts carry the operator right along with the load.

forklift truck

scraper

A new road is coming through! To make a level roadway, a scraper cuts through the top layers of earth. It carries away the dirt and rock in its big bowl. If there are holes or low spots, the scraper dumps out some of the dirt to fill them in.

grader

To smooth and flatten the roadway, a grader runs its big blade across the soil.

compactor

Then a compactor rolls along behind, packing down the dirt to make a hard surface.

cement mixer

float machine

paver

Now the roadway is ready to be paved. For concrete paving, several machines line up to form a "paving train." Wet concrete is dumped in front of the train. A paver spreads the concrete in an even layer. Then a float machine's long roller presses down and flattens the concrete. Last of all, the finisher float drags along a piece of heavy material to roughen the surface so that cars won't skid.

To show drivers where to drive, a line-painting machine marks the finished road. A burner inside the machine heats the paint so it will be easy to spray. The line painter sprays tiny glass beads that look like sand along with the paint to make the stripes shine at night. In only 30 seconds, the newly-painted stripes are dry. A truck follows the line painter to make sure no cars drive across the lines until they are dry.

finisher float

line painter

SLOW

logging machine

In the forest trees are cut down to be made into
lumber for furniture and houses. A logging
machine's metal arms hold the tree while its sharp
blades quickly cut through the trunk, close to the
ground. To replace the trees that have been cut
down, workers will plant new, young trees.

loader

skidder

The logs are dragged away by a skidder.
The skidder's deeply-treaded tires help it drive
over the roughest ground. Then a loader's big
pincers pick up the logs and load them onto
a truck.

Every fall the wheat farmer prepares the fields for next spring's planting. A small, strong tractor pulls a plow with fierce-looking claws that loosen the hard soil and turn under weeds and the stubble of old plants.

tractor

plow

Spring is planting time. Now the tractor pulls a grain drill. The drill's turning disks dig narrow trenches and drop wheat seeds and fertilizer into the ground.

grain drill

combine harvester

When it is time to pick the full-grown wheat, a combine harvester's whirling blades cut the long stalks and pull the wheat into the machine. Inside, paddles, blowers, and sieves separate the grain from the long stalks, or straw. Tanks hold the grain inside the harvester, and fans blow the straw out the back.

At a surface mine, miners dig away at the top layer of dirt and rock, called overburden, to get to the coal below. A crawler drill drives to the spot where the miners want to dig. The drill makes a deep hole, and workers carefully lower dynamite into it. Everyone gets out of the way. BOOM! The dynamite blast breaks up the rock into big chunks.

crawler

mining shovel

off-road dump truck

Now a mining shovel digs up the loosened rock and loads it into waiting trucks. Big off-road trucks can carry as much as 200 tons —a load as heavy as 200 cars! When the coal has been taken out of the mine, workers will replace the rock and soil and plants they took away.

Overburden can be cleared away even faster by a giant dragline. A dragline is a special crane with a bucket that scoops up rock and dirt. This one's bucket is as big as a 12-car garage! It is the world's largest moving land machine— a big work machine, helping people do a big job.

dragline